Perfect Paragraphs

A Step-By-Step Writing Guide

Written by Shelby Dersa

Cover art illustrated by Melissa Loxton

A HOMEMADE EDUCATION Press

Limit of Liability/Disclaimer of Warranty: While the publisher and author have used their best efforts in preparing this book, they make no representations or warranties with the respect to the accuracy of the contents of this book. The advice and strategies contained herein may not be suitable for your situation or your location. Neither the publisher or the author shall be liable for any inaccuracies.
Perfect Paragraphs: a step-by-step writing guide
Series: Homeschool Writing Workbooks
by Shelby Dersa
Paperback ISBN: 979-8-9882547-4-4
Printed in the United States of America.
A Homemade Education Press
ahomemadeeducation@gmail.com
ahomemadeeducationpress.com

Facebook.com/ahomemadeeducation (f)

ahomemadeeducationpress.com

Contents

Introduction

Knowing how to write a proper paragraph is crucial for writing essays, reports, narrative stories, etc. If you want to be a good writer, it starts with obtaining the skills to craft a great paragraph. This course tackles every aspect of writing a paragraph, giving examples and providing practice exercises along the way. Whether you are a student who is learning about paragraphs for the first time, a student who could improve their paragraghs, or one who is still struggleing the concept, this workbook is perfect for you.

Part One:

What Makes a Paragraph?

In this section, you'll learn about the parts that make up a paragraph. A paragraph is a group of sentences that focus on a single topic, argument, or idea. Every start to a new paragraph is marked by an indentation on the first line, which is usually five spaces from the left margin. By the end of part one, identifying the parts of a paragraph will be an easy task.

Anatomy of a Paragraph

Indentation

Topic Sentence

    If you want to visit a small town with big views, tour the streets of Port Huron, Michigan. The restaurants and cafes have a unique atmosphere with savory dishes and one-of-a-kind beverages. There are multiple museums including the oldest lighthouse grounds, the Thomas Edison Depot, and the Children's Discovery Center. Things to do include exploring the downtown shops and antique stores, taking a tour of the lake on the Huron Lady boat, or listening to outdoor concerts in front of the McMorran Plaza. Port Huron gives a close-knit community feel to its tourists, but provides numerous things to do and see.

Supporting Details

Closing Sentence

Anatomy of a Paragraph

Topic Sentence

This is the sentence that sets the stage for the entire paragraph. It serves two purposes: to catch the attention of the reader and to introduce the main idea of the entire paragraph as a whole.

Supporting Details

The supporting details make up the body of the paragraph. This part should consist of at least three sentences total that introduce three separate points, ideas, examples, or details that support the topic sentence.

Closing Sentence

This sentence provides a conclusion for the paragraph, bringing it to an end without abruptly stopping after the details are given. It is meant to reiterate what was said in the topic sentence while using different wording.

More Examples

Topic Sentence

There is no other dessert better than cake. Cake comes in multiple flavors, whether you are a chocolate lover, a fan of fruity tastes, or prefer the classic birthday cake, theres something for everyone. Cakes also take many forms, such as a five-tier wedding cake, a rectangle sheet cake, or a detailed theme of a child's favorite character or hobby. Lastly, cakes are great for any occasion because they can be eaten at fancy events or simple parties. Cakes make the best dessert for any time and any place.

Supporting Details

Closing Sentence

Topic Sentence

My summer break wasn't that adventurous, but I did get to explore the wilderness while camping for one week. When my family and I got to the campground, my eyes lit up. A stream and trees surrounded us. We hiked the trails while identifying animal tracks and types of plants. My favorite part was kayaking and swimming at the beach near our campsite. Even though we only drove four hours from our house, our trip felt like an exciting journey.

Supporting Details

8

Closing Sentence

Exercise: Match Up

A paragraph has been mixed up. Draw a line from each label to the matching text.

Topic Sentence

I might not be highly skilled at my new hobby, but I have accomplished my goal of learning how to crochet.

Supporting Details

I felt like learning a new hobby, so I chose crochet.

Closing Sentence

My grandma taught me some basic techniques one-on-one. Then I watched a ton of how-to videos online. Lastly, I joined a crochet club at my local library.

Part Two:

The Topic Sentence

The topic sentence is a statement that sets the stage for the rest of the paragraph. The purpose is to introduce the main idea to the reader, letting them know what is to follow. The topic sentence is usually the very first sentence in a simple paragraph, but can sometimes be a couple of sentences in when writing a fancier paragraph. We will explore both methods.

Examples of topic sentences:

- My favorite movie is The Land Before Time.
- Living in the rural country area is better than living in a big city.
- Bears are facinating mammals.
- Schools should only be open four days per week.
- Japan is an interesting country to visit.

What a Topic Sentence Looks Like in a Paragraph

Topic Sentence

Skateboarding is my favorite sport. I like that it can be done with others in a non-competitive way, or you can choose to participate in competitions as well. There are numerous tricks to try out and experiment with. I have made a lot of friends while practicing my skills as well.

Topic Sentence

Florida is a fun place to go on vacation. While I was there, I enjoyed trying many different foods. I also had fun swimming in the ocean. It was neat seeing palm trees for the first time, also.

Topic Sentence

The zoo is an awesome place to spend the day. People can learn about all kinds of animals, including exotic animals. The zoo has many special exhibits, such as the butterfly house or penguin sanctuary. I like seeing animals in real life that I've only ever been able to see on television.

Exercise: Find the Topic Sentence

Find the topic sentence in each paragraph and underline it.

1. <u>Mackinac Island is my favorite vacation spot.</u> A ferry must be taken to get there. Since no cars are allowed on the island, horse-drawn carriages fill the streets. There's lots of delicious food to eat, including their famous fudge. It was especially fun to visit the small shops around town and take home a souvenir.

2. <u>Cats are better pets than dogs.</u> Their owners do not have to let them outside multiple times per day. They usually don't need to be constantly attended to. Cats are also cuddly when they want to be.

3. <u>Libraries are a special place that should be appreciated.</u> With thousands of books available for free, anyone can have access to reading materials. Computers are also available for people who do not own one. On top of all that, many libraries offer free classes and events to participate in.

4. <u>I always enjoy going to my grandparents' house.</u> They are always offering me treats while I'm there. My grandma teaches me new things, like how to make bread. My grandpa and I birdwatch together.

5. <u>School days should be shorter.</u> Kids need more time to play outside and run around. They could also benefit from spending longer periods with their families. School shouldn't feel like a full-time job.

Exercise: Choose the Topic Sentence

After reading the details of each paragraph below, choose the best topic sentence for each one. Remember that the topic sentence is the main point of all the details.

1.   A ferry must be taken to get there. Since no cars are allowed on the island, horse-drawn carriages fill the streets. There's lots of delicious food to eat, including their famous fudge. It was especially fun to visit the small shops around town and take home a souvenir.

   A. I never want to go back to Macinac Island again.
   B. I recommend visiting Macinac Island.
   C. The restaurants on Macinac Island are the best part.

2.   Their owners do not have to let them outside multiple times per day. They usually don't need to be constantly attended to. Cats are also cuddly when they want to be.

   A. Cats are the friendliest pets.
   B. Cats are the worst pets.
   C. Cats are a low maintenance pet.

3.   With thousands of books available for free, anyone can have access to reading materials. Computers are also available for people who do not own one. On top of all that, many libraries offer free classes and events to participate in.

   A. Libraries are an asset to the community.
   B. Cities could not thrive without libraries.
   C. Libraries are the only place to get books for free.

Exercise: Choose the Topic Sentence

After reading the details of each paragraph below, choose the best topic sentence for each one. Remember that the topic sentence is the main point of all the details.

4. They are always offering me treats while I'm there. My grandma teaches me new things, like how to make bread. My grandpa and I bird watch together.

   A. My grandparents have a great house.
   B. My grandparents are nice people.
   C. Visiting my grandparents is always a fun time.

5. Kids need more time to play outside and run around. They could also benefit from spending longer periods with their families. School shouldn't feel like a full-time job.

   A. Kids need a longer recess time.
   B. Parents should consider homeschooling.
   C. Kids should not have to attend school at all.

6. He likes the same activities as I do. We live only one block away from each other. The best part is that he said we can hang out any time he's free.

   A. My cousin is a cool guy.
   B. My new lab partner is funny.
   C. I've known my best friend for years.
   D. My dad lives down the road from me.
   E. I met a new friend today.
   F. The mayor moved into my neighborhood.

Exercise: Write a Topic Sentence

Write a topic sentence based on the details given.

1. Going to college could lead to a career.
   Going to college could lead to more money earned later.
   Going to college could lead to meeting new people.

   _____

   _____

   _____

   _____

2. A gym membership provides someone with a place to exercise.
   A gym membership gives someone more equipment to use.
   A gym membership promotes a healthy lifestyle.

   _____

   _____

   _____

   _____

3. Tiny homes are eco-friendly.
   Tiny homes can be moved around so the owner can travel.
   Tiny homes can be more affordable than a house in the long run.

   _____

   _____

   _____

   _____

Exercise: Write a Topic Sentence

Write a topic sentence based on the details given.

1. Dogs are friendly companions.
   Dogs are good protectors.
   Dogs make people happy.

   _____

   _____

   _____

   _____

2. Swim lessons make people safe swimmers.
   Swim lessons are good exercise.
   Swim lessons can make someone more capable of saving someone else.

   _____

   _____

   _____

   _____

3. Animal shelters save dogs and cats.
   Animal shelters promote pet adoption.
   Animal shelters tend to the medical needs of animals brought in.

   _____

   _____

   _____

   _____

Exercise: Write a Topic Sentence

After reading the details of each paragraph below, write a topic sentence of your own.
Remember that the topic sentence is the main point of all the details.

1.   Ohio has an amusement park called Cedar Point. The most interesting
     restaurant the state has is called The Black Cat. Don't forget to visit the
     Rock and Roll Hall of Fame while you're there.

     _____

     _____

     _____

     _____

2.   Carrots, onions, and broccoli are some of the vegetables that I'm growing.
     In the summer, I sell some to the neighbors. When fall comes, I pick my last
     harvest and can't wait for the next gardening season to arrive.

     _____

     _____

     _____

     _____

3.   It sank on April 15th, 1912. An iceberg struck the ship at 11:40 PM.
     Despite having lifeboats on board, the Titanic did not have enough, and
     many sadly passed away during the tragedy.

     _____

     _____

     _____

     _____

Part Three:

Upgrade Any Topic Sentence

Any basic topic sentence can be easily upgraded into a finer piece of writing using one of many techniques. We'll explore four ways to do so in this section.

Upgrade techniques

- Write additional sentences that surround the topic sentence.
- Avoid announcements.
- Ask a question.
- State a fact or statistic.
- Use shock or excitement.
- Write a creative description with one or more sentences.

When a Topic Sentence Does Not Appear in the First Sentence

In the first section, you learned about simple topic sentences that were displayed immediately in the first sentence of the paragraph, followed by the supporting details of the paragraph. When writing a more advanced paragraph, writers can make their topic sentence come alive with additional sentences that either precede the topic sentence or follow it. When upgrading your topic sentence with the other techniques we will explore in this section, such as asking a question or stating an interesting fact, it's sometimes necessary to write more than one sentence before getting to the supporting details of the paragraph.

Take a look at the examples below. The topic sentences are underlined:

Wind blowing through my hair. Water spashing against my skin. The rush of excitement when a wave is coming. <u>Surfing is my favorite thing to do</u>. I like that it happens at the beach. I also like the new people I often meet while surfing. There's no pressure to compete, it's all in good fun. Surfing will be one of those things that never get old.

Have you ever wondered what it would be like to go some place sunny during winter break? <u>Florida is an amazing spot to go on vacation when it's cold back home.</u> While there, you can enjoy the beach all day long, see the everglades, or meet a dolphin. I enjoyed trying many different foods. I also had fun swimming in the ocean. It was neat seeing palm trees for the first time, too.

Accredited zoos have helped save at least thirty species of animals from extinction. <u>Some people believe that zoos force animals out of the wild, while many are actually helping them to survive.</u> When visiting the zoo, you may notice animals there that are particulary at risk, such as polar bears. Zoos give animals like the polar bear another chance at life when so many of its kind are actively dying due to climate change. Next time you're at the zoo, take notice of how many species are there that are on the brink of extinction.

Avoid Announcements

A common mistake that inexperienced writers make is when they use the topic sentence to state what they will be discussing in their paragraph. Making such announcements is not only unnecessary, but they appear as weak or even child-like. A topic sentence can immediately be upgraded by avoiding this mistake and getting directly to the point without using the author's actual voice.

Examples:

Wrong: I'm going to tell you all about polar bears.
Correct: Polar bears are not like any other bear on Earth.

Wrong: In this book report, I'll discuss The Mystery of the Missing Bike.
Correct: The Mystery of the Missing Bike is a novel full of suspensful twists and turns that will leave you on the edge of your chair.

Wrong: This report talks about my favorite place to visit.
Correct: Out of anywhere in the United States, I'd choose to go to Colorado over and over again.

Wrong: You should know about my best friend Ben.
Correct: It took ten years to make a good friend like Ben.

Wrong: Im going to list why school uniforms are not better than regular clothes.
Correct: Despite what some may think, school uniforms are not better than regular clothes.

Exercise: Fix the Topic Sentence

Rewrite each topic sentence below so that it does not directly announce to the reader what the paragraph will be about.

1.   I will discuss what I learned about Antarctica.

    _____

    _____

    _____

    _____

    _____

2.   Let me tell you why fruits are better desserts than other sugary treats.

    _____

    _____

    _____

    _____

    _____

3.   This paragraph will explain why hockey is my favorite sport.

    _____

    _____

    _____

    _____

    _____

Upgrade with Other Techniques

There is a correct way to write a topic sentence and then there is a better way. Any sentence can be upgraded with a little bit of effort and creativity. Take a look below at how they can be changed by using different techniques:

Basic sentence: Books will always be better than ebooks.
- **Ask a question:**

What's better than the feel of turning the pages to a real book?
- **State an interesting fact or statistic:**

Even though ebooks have been on the rise for years, people still prefer a real book.
- **Share an experience:**

The memories I have of my mother reading books to me as a child make me never want to switch from the feeling of a real book to an ebook.
- **Write a creative description:**

Imagine going to a bookstore to find that only descriptions of ebooks exist, and must be downloaded for purchase. <u>Despite the digital age we are in, that will most likely never happen because real people prefer real books.</u>

Basic sentence: Concerts are my favorite events to attend.
Ask a question: Have you ever heard your favorite band live in concert?
State an interesting fact or statistic: Five hundred people attend concerts every year in the United States.
Share an experience: The first concert I saw was in 2018 and it was also the first time I experienced anything like it.
Write a creative description: The crowd around you is full of energy. Everyone shares the same excitement as you do while waiting for the band to come out onto the stage. The lights begin flashing and the drums start to play. It's finally time to see your favorite songs come to life. <u>There's no experience like attending a concert.</u>

Exercise: Ask a Question

Rewrite each topic sentence below so that it asks an interesting question instead.

1. The highest mountain in America is Denali.

   _____

   _____

   _____

   _____

   _____

2. Everyone should make an effort to volunteer once in a while.

   _____

   _____

   _____

   _____

   _____

3. Children should have limited screen time.

   _____

   _____

   _____

   _____

   _____

Exercise: State an Interesting Fact

Research the topic on the internet to generate ideas, then rewrite each topic sentence below so that it states an interesting fact or statistic.

1. The highest mountain in America is Denali.

   _____

   _____

   _____

   _____

   _____

2. Everyone should make an effort to volunteer once in a while.

   _____

   _____

   _____

   _____

   _____

3. Children should have limited screen time.

   _____

   _____

   _____

   _____

   _____

Exercise: Share an Experience

Think about how to make the topic relatable to a personal experience, then rewrite the topic sentence. If you cannot think of anything, then make one up.

1.   The highest mountain in America is Denali.

_____

_____

_____

_____

_____

2.   Everyone should make an effort to volunteer once in a while.

_____

_____

_____

_____

3.   Children should have limited screen time.

_____

_____

_____

_____

Exercise: Use Creative Descriptions

For this technique, you'll write two to three sentences. The actual topic sentence can be in any of those sentences, even if it does not come first. Look at the answer key if more examples are needed.

1. Everyone should make an effort to volunteer once in a while.

    _____

    _____

    _____

    _____

    _____

    _____

    _____

    _____

2. Children should have limited screen time.

    _____

    _____

    _____

    _____

    _____

    _____

    _____

Exercise: Topic Sentence Prompts

Write a topic sentence based on the prompts given. Use any of the techniques previously learned about. Remember to only write the topic sentence, no other details.

1.   Tell about an embarrassing moment.

_____

_____

_____

_____

_____

2.   Explain the benefits of setting a goal to spend 1000 hours outside per year.

_____

_____

_____

_____

_____

3.   Write about your favorite animal

_____

_____

_____

_____

_____

Part Four:

The Supporting Details

The supporting details make up the body of the paragraph and should contain at least three sentences. These details should also be careful not to go off topic but stick to the main point that is being made in the topic sentence. They can include examples, reasons, quotes, personal experiences, etc.

Topic Sentence

Detail 1

Detail 2

Detail 3

Closing Sentence

What Supporting Details Look Like in a Paragraph

Supporting Details

Skateboarding is my favorite sport. <u>I like that it can be done with others in a non-competitive way, or you can choose to participate in competitions as well. There are numerous tricks to try out and experiment with. I have made a lot of friends while practicing my skills as well.</u> Skateboarding will probably always be my favorite sport.

Supporting Details

Florida is a fun place to go on vacation. <u>While I was there, I enjoyed trying many different foods. I also had fun swimming in the ocean. It was neat seeing palm trees for the first time, also.</u> What a wonderful state to spend a get-away.

Supporting Details

The zoo is an awesome place to spend the day. <u>People can learn about all kinds of animals, including exotic animals. The zoo has many special exhibits, such as the butterfly house or penguin sanctuary. I like seeing animals in real life that I've only ever been able to see on television.</u> There's always something new to see when <u>visiting the zoo.</u>

Exercise: Find the Supporting Details

Find the three sentences that contain the supporting details in each paragraph and underline them.

1.   Mackinac Island is my favorite vacation spot. A ferry must be taken to get there. Since no cars are allowed on the island, horse-drawn carriages fill the streets. There's lots of delicious food to eat, including their famous fudge. It was especially fun to visit the small shops around town and take home a souvenir. My family and I plan to go back next summer.

2.   Cats are better pets than dogs. Their owners do not have to let them outside multiple times per day. They usually don't need to be constantly attended to. Cats are also cuddly when they want to be. I will always choose a cat over a dog.

3.   Libraries are a special place that should be appreciated. With thousands of books available for free, anyone can have access to reading materials. Computers are also available for people who do not own one. On top of all that, many libraries offer free classes and events to participate in. I hope that libraries continue to exist for many years to come.

4.   I always enjoy going to my grandparents' house. They are always offering me treats while I'm there. My grandma teaches me new things, like how to make bread. My grandpa and I bird watch together. I'm sure I will miss the days spent at my grandparents' house.

5.   School days should be shorter. Kids need more time to play outside and run around. They could also benefit from spending longer periods with their families. Attending school shouldn't feel like a full-time job. Hopefully one day, schools will change their schedules.

Exercise: Choose the Supporting Details

Read the list of supporting details for each topic sentence. Underline the one detail that doesn't belong.

Topic sentence:
Route 66 is a hit roadtrip destination for Americans.

- Many choose road trips over airplanes for traveling.
- There are many attractions to see along the route.
- The route spans from Illinois to California.

Topic sentence:
Woodstock is a famous music event that occured in the 1960's.

- Young people traveled from other cities to attend.
- Traffic was so jammed up that many abandoned their cars on the side of the road and walked the rest of the way.
- Large music events are popular among youth.

Topic sentence:
You do not have to be published by a big company to become a successful author.

- Writers prefer to write for fun instead of for fame or money.
- Writers can start their own self-publishing business.
- Writers can grow an audience using social media.

Exercise: Choose the Supporting Details

Read the list of supporting details for each topic sentence. Underline the one detail that doesn't belong.

Topic sentence:

Gym class should not be mandatory after elementary school.

- Other ways to exercise should be offered, such as a walking club.
- Gym class should not be necessary to graduate.
- Children at this age should be able to choose to participate or not.

Topic sentence:

Every neighborhood would benefit from more bike lanes.

- Biking is better for environmental reasons.
- Citizens are safer when using bike lanes.
- Citizens can ride their bikes more easily.

Topic sentence:

Children don't need tablets.

- There are better toys to play with.
- Tablets can be addictive.
- Too much television is bad for kids.

Exercise: Choose the Supporting Details

Read the list of supporting details for each topic sentence. Underline the one detail that doesn't belong.

Topic sentence:
Spaghetti is an excellent dinner to serve when guests come over.

- It makes a large portion.
- Most people love spaghetti.
- Salad is a common side dish for spaghetti.

Topic sentence:
The Blue Water Bridge is an important piece of architecture.

- The bridge provides beautiful scenery to residents who live nearby.
- Truck drivers use the bridge to transport items to and from Canada.
- The bridge serves as a way for Americans to drive to Canada and vice versa.

Topic sentence:
Obtaining a drivers license at sixteen is beneficial for teenagers.

- Teenagers can drive to and from their jobs.
- Teenagers can learn to become responsible drivers.
- Teenagers are more likely to get into an accident than older drivers.

Exercise: Choose the Supporting Details

Choose the correct supporting details that go with the topic sentence.

Topic sentence:
Technological advancements are changing the future of our world for the better.

A.   As a result, jobs are being stolen from humans. From factories to grocery stores, robots will soon be in every place we look. How did society let it come to this?

B.   Robots are designed by people who have gone to college for mechanical or electrical engineering with a focus on robotics. A four-year degree is typically required. Many graduates choose to advance their careers by obtaining a master's degree.

C.   Robots have the potential to do things that are difficult for humans. For example, they can boost productivity across industries. They can also complete dangerous procedures or enhance healthcare through surgical assistance.

Exercise: Choose the Supporting Details

Choose the correct supporting details that go with the topic sentence.

Topic sentence:
Practicing music at a young age is beneficial if wanting to have a music career someday.

A.   This can range from voice lessons to instrument lessons. Many children participate in private lessons, which means one-on-one with an instructor. By the time they are teenagers, they may be ready to show off their skills.

B.   A music career is not for everyone. It can take many years to make it big in the business, if ever at all. Some may land a record deal only to lose it quickly if they do not become famous fast enough.

C.   Children might like to practice other skills as well, such as dancing, sports, and drawing. They should become more diverse instead of sticking to one talent. That way, a child is well-rounded.

Exercise: Choose the Supporting Details

Choose the correct supporting details that go with the topic sentence.

Topic sentence:
A flower garden brings joy all summer long.

A. It's a lot of work to tend to a garden. It may be fun for some gardeners, but it may be too much to take on for others who are not passionate about flowers. You must constantly water them and make sure they are thriving every day.

B. Eventhough it may be a lot of work, it keeps people busy in a productive way. Being able to see a flower bloom also gives them something to look forward to. By the end of the summer, it was all worth it.

C. The first step is to plan the location of where the flowers will be planted. Then, choose the proper flowers for that location. Lastly, tend to the flowers as needed.

Exercise: List Supporting Details

Make a list of three details that support each topic sentence.

Example

Topic sentence:

Puzzles can be a relaxing hobby.

- They keep you busy for hours.
- They take your mind off other things.
- They try to provide a stress-free activity.

Topic sentence:

There should be more after school activities offered besides sports.

_____

_____

_____

Topic sentence:

Neighborhood parks are beneficial to the children that reside in the area.

_____

_____

_____

Exercise: List Supporting Details

Make a list of three details that support each topic sentence.

Topic sentence:
Many interesting items can be found at an antique store.

_____

_____

_____

Topic sentence:
Hamburgers are a great food item to make at a cookout.

_____

_____

_____

Jewelry making is a hobby that can also be a side business.

_____

_____

_____

Exercise: List Supporting Details

Make a list of three details that support each topic sentence.

Topic sentence:
We should all protect the environment.

_____

_____

_____

Topic sentence:
Remember to have good manners when at a restaurant.

_____

_____

_____

Topic sentence:
There are three things you can do to live a healthy lifestyle.

_____

_____

_____

Exercise: List Supporting Details

Make a list of three details that support each topic sentence.

Topic sentence:
Fast food is not healthy.

_____

_____

_____

Topic sentence:
When going out shopping, it's important to set a budget.

_____

_____

_____

Topic sentence:
College should be free.

_____

_____

_____

Exercise: Turn it into a Paragraph

Make a list of three details that support each topic sentence, then rewrite it all in a paragraph. You do not have to include a concluding paragraph.

Topic sentence:
Children should not drink coffee.

-
-
-

_____

_____

_____

_____

_____

Topic sentence:
Teens should be allowed to drink coffee.

-
-
-

_____

_____

_____

_____

_____

41

Exercise: Turn it into a Paragraph

Make a list of three details that support each topic sentence, then rewrite it all in a paragraph. You do not have to include a concluding paragraph.

Topic sentence:
People should watch movies at home instead of going to the theater.

-
-
-

_____

_____

_____

_____

_____

Topic sentence:
There are many benefits of going hiking.

-
-
-

_____

_____

_____

_____

_____

42

Exercise: Turn it into a Paragraph

Make a list of three details that support each topic sentence, then rewrite it all in a paragraph. You do not have to include a concluding paragraph.

Topic sentence:
New York City is a popular New Year's Eve destination.

-
-
-

_____

_____

_____

_____

_____

Topic sentence:
Despite the cold weather, there are fun activities to do during the winter.

-
-
-

_____

_____

_____

_____

43

Exercise: Turn it into a Paragraph

Make a list of three details that support each topic sentence, then rewrite it all in a paragraph. You do not have to include a concluding paragraph.

Topic sentence:
Bigfoot is a controversial topic.

-
-
-

_____

_____

_____

_____

_____

Topic sentence:
Growing vegetables saves money.

-
-
-

_____

_____

_____

_____

_____

Part Five:

Upgrade the Supporting Details

The supporting details are the heart of the paragraph. They should be more than a simple list of ideas. The details tell a story about why your topic sentence is true. To better portray that story, different types of upgrades can be utilized.

Upgrade techniques

- Add transition words
- Add specific details: facts, statistics, dates, descriptions
- Add a variety of vocabulary: switch out bland words with better synonyms and eliminate repetitive words
- Add voices: expert quotes, author quotes, individual opinions, and different perspectives

Transitions

Within a paragraph, sentences move smoothly from one idea to the next by using transitions. Transitions are words or phrases that connect the sentences together so that it does not seem like random sentences are being written, but instead show how they relate to each other.

Example of transitions:

To give examples: for example, specifically, for instance, such as
- Sometimes wars end after many years, **for example**, the Cold War came to an unexpected end in 1972.

To show contrast: but, however, on the contrary, in contrast, at the same time, although, despite, in spite of, nevertheless
- **Despite** the rising cost of homes, people are still managing to buy a new house.

To show similarity: similarly, equally, likewise
- To become a massage therapist, you will need a certificate. **Similarly**, a manicurest needs one as well.

To show cause and effect: as a result, resulting in, consequently, therefore, so
- Many kids cannot afford school lunch, **as a result**, free lunch programs have been put in place.

To elaborate: also, furthermore, in addition, additionally, finally, first, next, then
- **In addition** to a new playground, the park will also receive a new drinking fountain.

To concede: while, although, even though, of course
- He went on to graduate high school, **even though** no one in his family ever has.

Exercise: Choose the Correct Transition

Fill in the blank with the best choice.

1. Sarah likes math, _____, she likes science more.

   A. so
   B. however
   C. even though

2. Choosing the right career is important, _____ you should finish school first.

   A. additionally
   B. for example
   C. but

3. The blue whale is gigantic, _____, it's the size of three school buses.

   A. for example
   B. similarly
   C. likewise

4. _____ the number of homeless people in our city, there is not enough affordable housing.
   A. on the contrary
   B. despite
   C. in addition to

Exercise: Choose the Correct Transition

Fill in the blank with the best choice.

1. _____, the rain started pouring down.

    A. first
    B. in conclusion
    C. suddenly

2. To make scrambled eggs, _____, you crack them, then add milk.

    A. next
    B. first
    C. suddenly

3. Sam made the cake, and _____, she made the decorations.

    A. even though
    B. although
    C. in addition

4. Other animals used to exist,_____, the mammoth once walked the Earth.

    A. for instance
    B. while
    C. however

Exercise: Insert a Transition

Fill in the blank with a transition of your choice. Refer to page 46 if needed.

1.   Matt loved to sing _____ he became a mechanic. His mom told him to follow his dreams _____ Matt wanted a more realistic career. _____ he did not not become a singer, he is still happy with his life.

2.   The oceans are constantly being pulluted _____ garbage often gets into the water in different ways. _____ volunteers and scientists are actively trying to clean up the oceans, it's hard to keep up with. _____ some people do not care.

3.   _____ there is a lot of useful information on the internet, there is a lot of bad content too. _____ fake news, unreliable information, and incredible websites continue to exist. _____ the amount of awareness, many people _____ get scammed.

3.   To make sausage soup, _____ add the broth. _____ add the vegetables. _____ add the sausage. _____ it is time to add the noodles. _____ it is not necessary, rolls are a good addition.

        Bookstores are a great place to discover new books. _____ libraries can be good for the same purpose. I love the bookstore, _____ the fantasy section.

Add Specific Details

When writing any kind of paragraph, it's beneficial to be specific. Specific information better supports the topic sentence and provides a more descriptive paragraph overall. Specific details include factual evidence, such as statistics, dates, events, research, names of people or places, etc. They can also tell more about the details of any topic or be more descriptive as opposed to making vague statements. Researching certain topics on the internet helps when specific details are unknown.

Examples:

Basic: Lexington is a lakeside town with thriving businesses.
Upgraded: Lexington is a lakeside town with popular businesses including Wimpy's Burgers, Christie's Antique Shop, and the Milk House Ice Cream Parlor.

Basic: Thomas Edison lived in Port Huron.
Upgraded: From age seven to fourteen, Thomas Edison lived in the town of Port Huron.

Basic: There are three kinds of popcorn at Betty's Bakeshop.
Upgraded: Caramel, toffee, and classic butter are three kinds of popcorn you'll find at Betty's Bakeshop.

Basic: The Bermuda Triangle is thought to be mysteriously dangerous.
Upgraded: Even though the Bermuda Triangle is thought to be mysteriously dangerous, scientists say that it's not anymore dangerous than other parts of the ocean.

Basic: A treehouse is a fun play area for children.
Upgraded: A treehouse is a place for a child to escape to in their own backyard.

Exercise: Add Specific Details

Use your imagination to make up specfic details related to the sentences below, then rewrite them.

Sperry's Movie House is a movie theater downtown.

_____

_____

_____

The carnival is coming to town.

_____

_____

_____

Marvin's Marvelous Mechanical Museum is a one-of-a-kind arcade.

_____

_____

_____

In the winter, the people of Mayville go ice skating.

_____

_____

_____

Exercise: Add Specific Details

Research the topics related to the sentences below, then add specfic details by rewriting the sentences.

The Grand Canyon receives plenty of visitors each year.

_____

_____

_____

The first man landed on the moon in 1969.

_____

_____

_____

Tulips bloom in the spring.

_____

_____

_____

Massage therapy has an excellent career outlook.

_____

_____

_____

Add a Variety of Vocabulary

When we converse with others, we tend to use much of the same vocabulary repeatedly. Your writing should be treated differently. It must be done with intention. That means purposefully not repeating words or phrases, combining sentences when possible, and omitting unnecessary words. Bland words can also be replaced with more interesting synonyms.

Examples:

Basic: People from surrounding towns drive to Lexington every summer to enjoy their beach town. The beach town is very popular.
Upgraded: People from surrounding towns drive to Lexington every summer. It's a popular beach town.

Basic: Thomas Edison lived in Port Huron.
Upgraded: Thomas Edison resided in Port Huron.

Basic: There are ten kinds of popcorn at Betty's Bakeshop.
Upgraded: There is a large variety of popcorn you'll find at Betty's Bakeshop.

Basic: The Bermuda Triangle is thought to be mysteriously dangerous. No one has solved the mystery yet as to why.
Upgraded: The Bermuda Triangle is thought to be mysteriously dangerous. It's a conundrum no one has solved.

Basic: A tree house is a lot of fun for children. They can play in it all day long. It is a magical place for children to hang out.
Upgraded: A treehouse is a magical place for children to have fun. They can play there all day.

Exercise: Add a Variety of Vocabulary

The sentences below have repeated words or phrases. Make changes by either switching out words or combining sentences.

The Grand Canyon receives plenty of visitors each year. Every year, people explore the canyon and take pictures of the view.

_____

_____

_____

The first man landed on the moon in 1969. The moon landing was astonishing.

_____

_____

_____

Tulips bloom in the spring and they always grow back and bloom again the next year as well.

_____

_____

_____

Massage therapy has an excellent career outlook. Not only does it have an excellent outlook, but it pays well too.

_____

_____

_____

Exercise: Add a Variety of Vocabulary

Rewrite each sentence to include more interesting vocabulary. Do this by choosing words already in the sentences and use the internet or a thesaurus to find synonyms.

The Grand Canyon gets a lot of visitors each year.

_____

_____

_____

After Neil Armstrong landed on the moon, more people continued to go there to see what was there.

_____

_____

_____

Tulips always grow in the springtime.

_____

_____

_____

Students in a massage therapy program can expect to make good money after finishing school.

_____

_____

_____

Add Voices

Bring paragraphs to life by adding voices. These can include direct and indirect quotes from others. The reason for doing this is to make your paragraph more credible, meaning it's more trustworthy or believable. Expert opinions, research studies, or news article pieces are all examples of someone else's voice. Direct quotes mean the exact words are taken from someone else. These quotes must include quotation marks around them. Indirect quotes are still sentences that have been taken from someone else but have been changed into your own words, also called paraphrasing.

Example of a direct quote within a sentence:

Quote: Paula Smith said, "the town of Lexington is one of the safest towns in Michigan."

Direct quote used within a paragraph: When choosing a town to move to in Michigan, safety may be one of your considering factors. According to the Mayor of Lexington, she said that, "Lexington is one of the safest towns in Michigan."

Indirect quote used within a paragraph: When choosing a town to move to in Michigan, safety may be one of your considering factors. The people of Lexington, including the mayor, say that it's one of the safest towns around.

Quote: Parenting Magazine said, "a tree house gives children a reason to play outside."

Direct quote used within a paragraph: A treehouse is a magical place for children to have fun. In fact, Parenting Magazine agrees. One of their articles stated, "a tree house gives children a reason to play outside in nature."

Indirect quote used within a paragraph: A tree house is a magical place for children to have fun. In fact, Parenting Magazine discusses how it can be beneficial because it promotes time spent in nature.

Exercise: Direct Quotes

Make up a sentence using the quotes provided.

Susie Thomas, a researcher: "Children are going outside less and less in each new generation."

_____

_____

_____

The Port Huron Times newspaper: "The Crazy Pins Bowling Alley is having a grand opening on Saturday."

_____

_____

_____

The governor: "All children will receive free school lunch for the upcoming school year."

_____

_____

_____

A scientist: "Bees are important for the planet."

_____

_____

_____

Exercise: Indirect Quotes

Make up a sentence by rephrasing the quotes below into your own words. A quotation mark is not needed, but you should still mention who said the quote.

Susie Thomas, a researcher: "Children are going outside less and less in each new generation."

_____

_____

_____

The Port Huron Times newspaper: "The Crazy Pins Bowling Alley is having a grand opening on Saturday."

_____

_____

_____

The governor: "All children will receive free school lunch for the upcoming school year."

_____

_____

_____

A scientist: "Bees are important for the planet."

_____

_____

_____

Exercise: Find Your Own Quotes

Two topics are provided below. Research each topic and write one direct quote and one indirect quote for each.

Robotics is potentially a smart career choice.

_____

_____

_____

_____

_____

_____

Playing video games teaches children important skills.

_____

_____

_____

_____

_____

_____

Part Six:

The Closing Sentence

The closing sentence does not include any new details, but summarizes the main idea of the paragraph. It basically is an opportunity to restate the topic sentence by using different words. The purpose of the closing sentence is to wrap up the paragraph without ending it abruptly.

Upgrade Ideas:

- Share an opinion
- Ask a question
- Add a future thought

Examples:

Topic sentence: Bees are important for our planct and we must protect them.

Share an opinion in the closing sentence: Bees are the most important insect on Earth.

Ask a question in the closing sentence: How will you help protect the bees?

Add a future thought in the closing sentence: Imagine our world if we stopped protecting the bees.

Exercise: Choose the Closing Sentence

Read each paragraph then choose the best closing sentence.

1. What fun it is to visit my grandparents. They offer me treats while I'm there. My grandma teaches me new things, like how to make bread. My grandpa and I bird watch together.

   A. It's always a great time at my grandparents' house.
   B. My grandpa is a smart man.
   C. My grandparents know a lot of things.

2. Think of the benefits of no homework after school. Children could benefit from spending longer periods with their families. They could have more time for hobbies. They would also be able to see their friends more often.

   A. Kids need a longer recess time.
   B. How could you benefit from no more homework?
   C. More time to do other things is important.

3. The coolest kid moved into the house down the street. He likes the same activities as I do. He is going to go to my homeschool co-op. The best part is that he said we can hang out any time he's free.

   A. I can't believe I have an awesome new friend who lives a block away.
   B. We're going to hang out tomorrow.
   C. We have many plans made already.

Exercise: Write a Closing Sentence

Read the paragraphs below and add your own closing sentence.

Spaghetti is an excellent dinner to serve when guests come over. It makes a large portion, most people love it, and you can add yummy sides like garlic bread.

_____

_____

_____

The Blue Water Bridge is an important piece of architecture. It provides a route of transportation for shipping trucks traveling from the U.S. to Canada. It allows tourists to visit America. It also lets Americans go to Canada and see Niagara Falls.

_____

_____

_____

Golden retrievers are a popular family dog. They enjoy being around children. They are generally friendly. They also like to play.

_____

_____

_____

Exercise: Write a Closing Sentence

Read the paragraphs below and add your own closing sentence.

Summer camp is a place I look forward to going every year. I see old friends. We go on hikes. There are always crafts, archery, swimming, fishing, and campfires.

_____

_____

_____

I was worried about starting my first job, but it turned out to be a lot of fun. I learned new skills. I met new people. The job also helped build my confidence, so I won't be as nervous for my next job.

_____

_____

_____

Everyone is excited about the school dance coming up. There will be a live band. Food and drinks are going to be available. We all have to dress up too.

_____

_____

_____

Exercise: Write a Closing Sentence

Read the paragraphs below and add your own closing sentence.

The boardwalk is where teenagers like to hang out on summer nights. They park their cars along the river. Some turn the music up loud. Everyone talks and mingles by the parking lot.

_____

_____

_____

The Sandusky drive-in is the last standing outdoor theater in Michigan. Every summer, people from all around drive there for the experience. The concession stand has food and drinks. There are two movies that play back to back.

_____

_____

_____

Making candles is a hobby that some crafty people might enjoy. It's a skill that must be learned. You can give them away as gifts. They also make nice decorations for yourself.

_____

_____

_____

Part Seven:

Writing Paragraphs

You now have the skills to put what you know to the test. The following pages can be used to practice writing different kinds of paragraphs, including informative, persuasive, and narrative. A checklist of key points is included on the next page. Use it as your guide while completing the paragraph exercises.

Writing Guide

Topic Sentence:
States the main idea of the paragraph. It tells the reader what the paragraph will be about.

Upgrade Ideas:
- Add a surprising fact or statistic
- Add excitement
- Ask an interesting question
- Write a creative description

Supporting Details:
Contains at least three details to support the topic sentence.

Upgrade Ideas:
- Use transition words: review page 46
- Include specfic details: facts and descriptions
- Add a variety of vocabulary: switch out boring words for more interesting synonyms. Throw out repetitive words.
- Add voices: direct quotes and indirect quotes

Closing Sentence:
Restate the topic sentence in a different way.

Upgrade Ideas:
- Ask a question
- Share an opinion
- State a future thought

Exercise: Informative Paragraph

Write a paragraph about an animal of your choosing.

Topic sentence: _____

_____

Three details

- _____
- _____
- _____

Closing sentence: _____

_____

_____

_____

_____

_____

_____

_____

_____

67

Exercise: Persuasive Paragraph

Think of a new law that you think your country should have. Write a paragraph persuading others to believe the same.

Topic sentence: _____

_____

Three details

- _____
- _____
- _____

Closing sentence: _____

_____

_____

_____

_____

_____

_____

_____

_____

_____

Exercise: Informative Paragraph

Write about a topic that interests you.

Topic sentence: _____

_____

Three details

- _____
- _____
- _____

Closing sentence: _____

_____

_____

_____

_____

_____

_____

_____

_____

_____

Exercise: Narrative Paragraph

Write a paragraph describing the coolest place you have been.

Topic sentence: _____
_____

Three details

- _____
- _____
- _____

Closing sentence: _____

_____

_____

_____

_____

_____

_____

_____

_____

_____

70

Answer Key

Exercise: Match Up

A paragraph has been mixed up. Draw a line from each label to the matching text.

Topic Sentence

Supporting Details

Closing Sentence

I might not be highly skilled at my new hobby, but I have accomplished my goal of learning how to crochet.

I felt like learning a new hobby, so I chose crochet.

My grandma taught me some basic techniques one-on-one. Then I watched a ton of how-to videos online. Lastly, I joined a crochet club at my local library.

9

Exercise: Find the Topic Sentence

Find the topic sentence in each paragraph and underline it.

1. <u>Mackinac Island is my favorite vacation spot.</u> A ferry must be taken to get there. Since no cars are allowed on the island, horse-drawn carriages fill the streets. There's lots of delicious food to eat, including their famous fudge. It was especially fun to visit the small shops around town and take home a souvenir.

2. <u>Cats are better pets than dogs.</u> Their owners do not have to let them outside multiple times per day. They usually don't need to be constantly attended to. Cats are also cuddly when they want to be.

3. <u>Libraries are a special place that should be appreciated.</u> With thousands of books available for free, anyone can have access to reading materials. Computers are also available for people who do not own one. On top of all that, many libraries offer free classes and events to participate in.

4. <u>I always enjoy going to my grandparents' house.</u> They are always offering me treats while I'm there. My grandma teaches me new things, like how to make bread. My grandpa and I birdwatch together.

5. <u>School days should be shorter. Kids need more time to play outside and run around.</u> They could also benefit from spending longer periods with their families. School shouldn't feel like a full-time job.

12

Exercise: Choose the Topic Sentence

After reading the details of each paragraph below, choose the best topic sentence for each one. Remember that the topic sentence is the main point of all the details.

1. A ferry must be taken to get there. Since no cars are allowed on the island, horse-drawn carriages fill the streets. There's lots of delicious food to eat, including their famous fudge. It was especially fun to visit the small shops around town and take home a souvenir.

   A. I never want to go back to Macinac Island again.
   B. I recommend visiting Macinac Island.
   C. The restaurants on Macinac Island are the best part.

2. Their owners do not have to let them outside multiple times per day. They usually don't need to be constantly attended to. Cats are also cuddly when they want to be.

   A. Cats are the friendliest pets.
   B. Cats are the worst pets.
   C. Cats are a low maintenance pet.

3. With thousands of books available for free, anyone can have access to reading materials. Computers are also available for people who do not own one. On top of all that, many libraries offer free classes and events to participate in.

   A. Libraries are an asset to the community.
   B. Cities could not thrive without libraries.
   C. Libraries are the only place to get books for free.

13

74

Exercise: Choose the Topic Sentence

After reading the details of each paragraph below, choose the best topic sentence for each one. Remember that the topic sentence is the main point of all the details.

4.   They are always offering me treats while I'm there. My grandma teaches me new things, like how to make bread. My grandpa and I bird watch together.

  A. My grandparents have a great house.
  B. My grandparents are nice people.
  C. Visiting my grandparents is always a fun time.

5.   Kids need more time to play outside and run around. They could also benefit from spending longer periods with their families. School shouldn't feel like a full-time job.

  A. Kids need a longer recess time.
  B. Parents should consider homeschooling.
  C. Kids should not have to attend school at all.

6.   He likes the same activities as I do. We live only one block away from each other. The best part is that he said we can hang out any time he's free.

  A. My cousin is a cool guy.
  B. My new lab partner is funny.
  C. I've known my best friend for years.
  D. My dad lives down the road from me.
  E. I met a new friend today.
  F. The mayor moved into my neighborhood.

14

Exercise: Write a Topic Sentence

Write a topic sentence based on the details given.

---

1.   Going to college could lead to a career.   **Possible answers**
     Going to college could lead to more money earned later.
     Going to college could lead to meeting new people.

     High school graduates might want to consider going to college.

2.   A gym membership provides someone with a place to exercise.
     A gym membership gives someone more equipment to use.
     A gym membership promotes a healthy lifestyle.

     A gym membership is worth the investment.

3.   Tiny homes are eco-friendly.
     Tiny homes can be moved around so the owner can travel.
     Tiny homes can be more affordable than a house in the long run.

     Tiny homes are on the rise.

15

Exercise: Write a Topic Sentence

Write a topic sentence based on the details given.   **Possible answers**

1.   Dogs are friendly companions.
       Dogs are good protectors.
       Dogs make people happy.
       Dogs make good family pets.
       _____
       _____
       _____

2.   Swim lessons make people safe swimmers.
       Swim lessons are good exercise.
       Swim lessons can make someone more capable of saving someone else.

       Everyone should take swim lessons.
       _____
       _____
       _____

3.   Animal shelters save dogs and cats.
       Animal shelters promote pet adoption.
       Animal shelters tend to the medical needs of animals brought in.
       Animal shelters are important to have in the community.
       _____
       _____
       _____

16

Exercise: Write a Topic Sentence

After reading the details of each paragraph below, write a topic sentence of your own.
Remember that the topic sentence is the main point of all the details.

Possible answers

1. Ohio has an amusement park called Cedar Point. The most interesting restaurant the state has is called The Black Cat. Don't forget to visit the Rock and Roll Hall of Fame while you're there.

   Ohio is a fun place for a day trip.

2. Carrots, onions, and broccoli are some of the vegetables that I'm growing. In the summer, I sell some to the neighbors. When fall comes, I pick my last harvest and can't wait for the next gardening season to arrive.

   A vegetable garden brings a lot of joy.

3. It sank on April 15th, 1912. An iceberg struck the ship at 11:40 PM. Despite having lifeboats on board, the Titanic did not have enough, and many sadly passed away during the tragedy.

   Many believe the devastation of the Titanic was avoidable.

17

Exercise: Fix the Topic Sentence

Rewrite each topic sentence below so that it does not directly announce to the reader what the paragraph will be about.

Possible answers

1. I will discuss what I learned about Antarctica.

   There is much to be learned about Antartica.

2. Let me tell you why fruits are better desserts than other sugary treats.

   Get ready to find out why fruits make better desserts than sugary treats.

3. This paragraph will explain why hockey is my favorite sport.

   When thinking about what sport us the best, hockey comes first.

21

Exercise: Ask a Question

Rewrite each topic sentence below so that it asks an interesting question instead.

Possible answers

1. The highest mountain in America is Denali.

    _____

    Do you have any idea what the highest mountain in the world is?

    _____

    _____

    _____

2. Everyone should make an effort to volunteer once in a while.

    _____

    When is the last time you have volunteered?

    _____

    _____

    _____

3. Children should have limited screen time.

    _____

    Do you know why researchers recommend putting a limit on screen time?

    _____

    _____

    _____

23

Exercise: State an Interesting Fact

Research the topic on the internet to generate ideas, then rewrite each topic sentence below so that it states an interesting fact or statistic.

Possible answers

1.   The highest mountain in America is Denali.

_____

Reaching 20,310 feet tall, Mount Denali is the highest mountain in
America.
_____

_____

_____

2.   Everyone should make an effort to volunteer once in a while.

_____

On average, 28 percent of Americans volunteer once per year, a number we
should try to raise.
_____

_____

_____

3.   Children should have limited screen time.

_____

Research shows that unlimited screen time can be detrimental to children,
leading experts to believe it should be limited.
_____

_____

_____

24

81

Exercise: Share an Experience

Think about how to make the topic relatable to a personal experience, then rewrite the topic sentence. If you cannot think of anything, then make one up.

Possible answers

1. The highest mountain in America is Denali.

   I was blown away when I saw the higest mountain in America.

   _____

   _____

   _____

   _____

2. Everyone should make an effort to volunteer once in a while.

   After a day of volunteering, I felt good inside, making me think about how everyone should make an effort to do so too.

   _____

   _____

   _____

3. Children should have limited screen time.

   _____

   When I did not have a limit on screen time, I became addicted, which led me to believe that screen time should be limited for children.

   _____

   _____

25

Exercise: Use Creative Descriptions

For this technique, you'll write two to three sentences. The actual topic sentence can be in any of those sentences, even if it does not come first. Look at the answer key if more examples are needed.

Possible answer

1. Everyone should make an effort to volunteer once in a while.

   The animal shelter is full of dogs waiting for homes. They are resting in small cages, lonely and afraid. When someone walks in, some begin to wag their rails in excitement, while others bark for attention. The person they are seeing is a volunteer, someone who they look forawrd to seeing every day. Everyone should make an effort to volunteer once in a while because it can make a huge difference for someone else.

2. Children should have limited screen time.

26

83

Exercise: Topic Sentence Prompts

Write a topic sentence based on the prompts given. Use any of the techniques previously learned about. Remember to only write the topic sentence, no other details.

1.   Tell about an embarrassing moment.   **Possible answers**

   Everyone has had embarrassing moments, but mine tops many others, I'm sure.

   _____

   _____

   _____

2.   Explain the benefits of setting a goal to spend 1000 hours outside per year.

   Have you ever set a goal to spend 1000 hours outside like others are currently doing?.

   _____

   _____

   _____

3.   Write about your favorite animal

   Hedgehogs are not a typical animal, that's why I want one.

   _____

   _____

   _____

   _____

27

Exercise: Find the Supporting Details

Find the three sentences that contain the supporting details in each paragraph and underline them.

1. Mackinac Island is my favorite vacation spot. A ferry must be taken to get there. Since no cars are allowed on the island, horse-drawn carriages fill the streets. There's lots of delicious food to eat, including their famous fudge. It was especially fun to visit the small shops around town and take home a souvenir. My family and I plan to go back next summer.

2. Cats are better pets than dogs. Their owners do not have to let them outside multiple times per day. They usually don't need to be constantly attended to. Cats are also cuddly when they want to be. I will always choose a cat over a dog.

3. Libraries are a special place that should be appreciated. With thousands of books available for free, anyone can have access to reading materials. Computers are also available for people who do not own one. On top of all that, many libraries offer free classes and events to participate in. I hope that libraries continue to exist for many years to come.

4. I always enjoy going to my grandparents' house. They are always offering me treats while I'm there. My grandma teaches me new things, like how to make bread. My grandpa and I bird watch together. I'm sure I will miss the days spent at my grandparents' house.

5. School days should be shorter. Kids need more time to play outside and run around. They could also benefit from spending longer periods with their families. Attending school shouldn't feel like a full-time job. Hopefully one day, schools will change their schedules.

30

Exercise: Choose the Supporting Details

Read the list of supporting details for each topic sentence. Underline the one detail that doesn't belong.

Topic sentence:
Route 66 is a hit roadtrip destination for Americans.

- <u>Many choose road trips over airplanes for traveling.</u>
- There are many attractions to see along the route.
- The route spans from Illinois to California.

Topic sentence:
Woodstock is a famous music event that occured in the 1960's.

- Young people traveled from other cities to attend.
- Traffic was so jammed up that many abandoned their cars on the side of the road and walked the rest of the way.
- <u>Large music events are popular among youth.</u>

Topic sentence:
You do not have to be published by a big company to become a successful author.

- <u>Writers prefer to write for fun instead of for fame or money.</u>
- Writers can start their own self-publishing business.
- Writers can grow an audience using social media.

31

Exercise: Choose the Supporting Details

Read the list of supporting details for each topic sentence. Underline the one detail that doesn't belong.

Topic sentence:
Gym class should not be mandatory after elementary school.

- Other ways to exercise should be offered, such as a walking club.
- Gym class should not be necessary to graduate.
- Children at this age should be able to choose to participate or not.

Topic sentence:
Every neighborhood would benefit from more bike lanes.

- Biking is better for environmental reasons.
- Citizens are safer when using bike lanes.
- Citizens can ride their bikes more easily.

Topic sentence:
Children don't need tablets.

- There are better toys to play with.
- Tablets can be addictive.
- Too much television is bad for kids.

32

Exercise: Choose the Supporting Details

Read the list of supporting details for each topic sentence. Underline the one detail that doesn't belong.

Topic sentence:
Spaghetti is an excellent dinner to serve when guests come over.

- It makes a large portion.
- Most people love spaghetti.
- <u>Salad is a common side dish for spaghetti.</u>

Topic sentence:
The Blue Water Bridge is an important piece of architecture.

- <u>The bridge provides beautiful scenery to residents who live nearby.</u>
- Truck drivers use the bridge to transport items to and from Canada.
- The bridge serves as a way for Americans to drive to Canada and vice versa.

Topic sentence:
Obtaining a drivers license at sixteen is beneficial for teenagers.

- Teenagers can drive to and from their jobs.
- Teenagers can learn to become responsible drivers.
- <u>Teenagers are more likely to get into an accident than older drivers.</u>

33

Exercise: Choose the Supporting Details

Choose the correct supporting details that go with the topic sentence.

Topic sentence:
Technological advancements are changing the future of our world for the better.

A. As a result, jobs are being stolen from humans. From factories to grocery stores, robots will soon be in every place we look. How did society let it come to this?

B. Robots are designed by people who have gone to college for mechanical or electrical engineering with a focus on robotics. A four-year degree is typically required. Many graduates choose to advance their careers by obtaining a master's degree.

C. Robots have the potential to do things that are difficult for humans. For example, they can boost productivity across industries. They can also complete dangerous procedures or enhance healthcare through surgical assistance.

34

Exercise: Choose the Supporting Details

Choose the correct supporting details that go with the topic sentence.

Topic sentence:
Practicing music at a young age is beneficial if wanting to have a music career someday.

A. This can range from voice lessons to instrument lessons. Many children participate in private lessons, which means one-on-one with an instructor. By the time they are teenagers, they may be ready to show off their skills.

B. A music career is not for everyone. It can take many years to make it big in the business, if ever at all. Some may land a record deal only to lose it quickly if they do not become famous quickly enough.

C. Children might like to practice other skills as well, such as dancing, sports, and drawing. They should become more diverse instead of sticking to one talent. That way, a child is well-rounded.

35

Exercise: Choose the Supporting Details

Choose the correct supporting details that go with the topic sentence.

Topic sentence:
A flower garden brings joy all Summer long.

A.   It's a lot of work to tend to a garden. It may be fun for some gardeners, but it may be too much to take on for others who are not passionate about flowers. You must constantly water them and make sure they are thriving every day.

B.   Eventhough it may be a lot of work, it keeps people busy in a productive way. Being able to see a flower bloom also gives them something to look forward to. By the end of the Summer, it was all worth it.

C.   The first step is to plan the location of where the flowers will be planted. Then, choose the proper flowers for that location. Lastly, tend to the flowers as needed.

36

Exercise: List Supporting Details

Make a list of three details that support each topic sentence.

Possible answers

Example

Topic sentence:

Puzzles can be a relaxing hobby.

- They keep you busy for hours.
- They take your mind off other things.
- They try to provide a stress-free activity.

Topic sentence:

There should be more after school activities offered besides sports.

- Not everyone likes sports.
- Kids can find out about other hobbies they may be interested in.
- More kids could have something to do after school.

Topic sentence:

Neighborhood parks are beneficial to the children that reside in the area.

- Some kids do not have a big yrd to play in.
- Kids can make new friends in their neighborhood.
- Parks can give a child a place to get some exercise.

37

Exercise: List Supporting Details

Make a list of three details that support each topic sentence.

Possible answers

Topic sentence:
Many interesting items can be found at an antique store.

- Nostalgic items

- Valuable items

- Collectable items

Topic sentence:
Hamburgers are a great food item to make at a cookout.

- They are a classic American food item.

- Most people enjoy hamburgers.

- People can expect hamburgers at a cookout.

Jewelry making is a hobby that can also be a side business.

- It can be sold online.

- It can be sold at craft shows.

- It can be sold to friends and family.

38

Exercise: List Supporting Details

Make a list of three details that support each topic sentence.

___

Possible answers

Topic sentence:
We should all protect the environment.

- Animals will benefit from it.

- Future generations will benefit from it.

- Our drinking water and air quality will benefit from it.

Topic sentence:
Remember to have good manners when at a restaurant.

- It enhances social experiences.

- It shows respect.

- It provides a positive dining experience for everyone.

Topic sentence:
There are three things you can do to live a healthy lifestyle.

- Exercise

- Eat healthy

- Practice mindfulness

39

Exercise: List Supporting Details

Make a list of three details that support each topic sentence.

Possible answers

Topic sentence:
Fast food is not healthy.

- It's full of additives.

- A lot of it is fried in oil.

- It's typically high in calories.

Topic sentence:
When going out shopping, it's important to set a budget.

- To make sure you don't over spend.

- To make sure there is enough left for bills.

- To make shopping simpler.

Topic sentence:
College should be free.

- So that everyone can gain a degree.

- So that everyone can have more job opportunities.

- So that people are not in debt the rest of their lives.

40

Exercise: Turn it into a Paragraph

Make a list of three details that support each topic sentence, then rewrite it all in a paragraph. You do not have to include a concluding paragraph.

Topic sentence:
Children should not drink coffee.

Possible answers

- It can make them anxious.
- It can affect sleep.
- It can affect their heart.

Children should not be drinking coffee. Not only can it affect their sleep, but it can make them anxious or increase their heart rate.

Topic sentence:
Teens should be allowed to drink coffee.

- It increases alertness.
- It can be a social activity.
- It contains antioxidants.

Despite the negative reasons, coffee can be beneficial to teens, so they should be allowed to drink it in moderate amounts. Coffee can increase alertness, making them be able to concentrate in school. Drinking it can also be used as a social activity, such as at cafes. Lastly, coffee contains healthy antioxidants.

41

Exercise: Choose the Correct Transition

Fill in the blank with the best choice.

---

1. Sarah likes math, _____, she likes science more.

    A. so
    B. however
    C. even though

2. Choosing the right career is important, _____ you should finish school first.

    A. additionally
    B. for example
    C. but

3. The blue whale is gigantic, _____, it's the size of three school buses.

    A. for example
    B. similarly
    C. likewise

4. _____ the number of homeless people in our city, there is not enough affordable housing.
    A. on the contrary
    B. despite
    C. in addition to

47

Exercise: Choose the Correct Transition

Fill in the blank with the best choice.

---

1.   _____, the rain started pouring down.

      A. first
      B. in conclusion
      C. suddenly

2.   To make scrambled eggs, _____, you crack them, then add milk.

      A. next
      B. first
      C. suddenly

3.   Sam made the cake, and _____, she made the decorations.

      A. even though
      B. although
      C. in addition

4.   Other animals used to exist,_____, the mammoth once walked the Earth.

      A. for instance
      B. while
      C. however

48

Exercise: Insert a Transition

Fill in the blank with a transition of your choice. Refer to page 46 if needed.

1. Matt loved to sing **,but** he became a mechanic. His mom told him to follow his dreams **,however,** Matt wanted a more realistic career. **Although** he did not not become a singer, he is still happy with his life.

2. The oceans are constantly being pulluted **,for example** garbage often gets into the water in different ways. **Even though** volunteers and scientists are actively trying to clean up the oceans, it's hard to keep up with. **However,** some people do not care.

3. **Even though** there is a lot of useful information on the internet, there is a lot of bad content too. **For instance,** fake news, unreliable information, and incredible websites continue to exist. **Despite** the amount of awareness, many people **as a result** get scammed.

3. To make sausage soup, **first,** add the broth. **Next,** add the vegetables. **Then,** add the sausage. **Finally,** it is time to add the noodles. **Although** it is not necessary, rolls are a good addition.

    Bookstores are a great place to discover new books. **However,** libraries can be good for the same purpose. I love the bookstore, **specifically** the fantasy section.

49   Possible answers

Exercise: Add Specific Details

Use your imagination to make up specfic details related to the sentences below, then rewrite them.

Sperry's Movie House is a movie theater downtown.

<u>Sperry's Movie House is a popular movie theater downtown with three</u> stories, a restaurant, and an arcade.

The carnival is coming to town.

<u>The Mkinnley carnival is coming to town during fourth of July week.</u>

Marvin's Marvelous Mechanical Museum is a one-of-a-kind arcade.

<u>An arcade that would blow your mind is the Marvin's Marvelous</u> Mechanical Museum, which features a large collection of pinball machines.

In the Winter, the people of Mayville go ice skating.

<u>The Winter season brings out the people of Mayville for ice skating on the</u> old ice rink that is located in the heart of their town.

51

Exercise: Add Specific Details

Research the topics related to the sentences below, then add specfic details by rewriting the sentences.

Possible answers

The Grand Canyon receives plenty of visitors each year.

The Grand Canyon, which is made up of 1.8 billion year old igneous and metamorphic rocks, sees around 5 million visitors each year.

The first man landed on the moon in 1969.

To wrap up the 1960s, NASA had a mission to land the first man on the moon, which finally occurred in 1969.

Tulips bloom in the Spring.

Known as early bloomers, tulips appear during March as Spring begins.

Massage therapy has an excellent career outlook.

Growing faster than most career choices, massage therapy is expected to have an excellent outlook for available jobs during the course of the next decade.

52

Exercise: Add a Variety of Vocabulary

The sentences below have repeated words or phrases. Make changes by either switching out words or combining sentences.

Possible answers

The Grand Canyon receives plenty of visitors each year. Every year, people explore the canyon and take pictures of the view.

The Grand Canyon receives plenty of visitors each year who explore and take pictures.

The first man landed on the moon in 1969. The moon landing was astonishing.

The first man landed on the moon in 1969 and it was astonishing.

Tulips bloom in the spring and they always grow back and bloom again the next year as well.

Tulips bloom in the spring and they are perennials, meaning they grow back year after year.

Massage therapy has an excellent career outlook. Not only does it have an excellent outlook, but it pays well too.

Not only does massage therapy have an excellent career outlook, but it pays well too.

54

Exercise: Add a Variety of Vocabulary

Rewrite each sentence to include more interesting vocabulary. Do this by choosing words already in the sentences and use the internet or a thesaurus to find synonyms.

The Grand Canyon gets a lot of visitors each year. **Possible answers**

The Grand Canyon receives a numerous amount of visitors each year.

_____

_____

After Neil Armstrong landed on the moon, more people continued to go there to see what was there.

Neil Armstrong, who landed on the moon, paved the way for
astronauts to come.

_____

_____

Tulips always grow in the springtime.

Tulips are expected to grow every spring season.

_____

_____

Students in a massage therapy program can expect to make good money after finishing school.

Students who attend a massage therapy program can expect to make a decent
amount of money after completing school.

_____

_____

55

Exercise: Direct Quotes

Make up a sentence using the quotes provided.

Possible answers

Susie Thomas, a researcher: "Children are going outside less and less in each new generation."

Parents should be concerned with the number of hours their children spend outside. According to Susie Thomas, a researcher, "children are going outside less and less in each new generation."

The Port Huron Times newspaper: "The Crazy Pins Bowling Alley is having a grand opening on Saturday."

Many children in town will be excited to have something to do this Fall, as the Port Huron Times newspaper reports that "the Crazy Pins Bowling Alley is having a grand opening on Saturday."

The governor: "All children will recieve free school lunch for the upcoming school year."

Money will be a little less tight this coming school year. For instance, the governor announced that "all children will receive free school lunch for the upcoming school year."

A scientist: "Bees are important for the planet."

According to scientists, "bees are important for the planet," so we should protect them.

57

104

Exercise: Indirect Quotes

Make up a sentence by rephrasing the quotes below into your own words. A quotation mark is not needed, but you should still mention who said the quote.

Possible answers

Susie Thomas, a researcher: "Children are going outside less and less in each new generation."

Susie Thomas, a researcher, discusses how children are going outside less frequently with each passing generation.

The Port Huron Times newspaper: "The Crazy Pins Bowling Alley is having a grand opening on Saturday."

The Port Huron Times newspaper wrote an article about how the Crazy Pins Bowling Alley will have a special grand opening this weekend.

The governor: "All children will recieve free school lunch for the upcoming school year."

Parents can get excited about saving money this school year because the governor announced that every student in our state will receive free school lunch.

A scientist: "Bees are important for the planet."

Scientists frequently talk about how vital bees are to society, so we should protect them.

58

Exercise: Choose the Closing Sentence

Read each paragraph then choose the best closing sentence.

1.   What fun it is to visit my grandparents. They offer me treats while I'm
       there. My grandma teaches me new things, like how to make bread. My
       grandpa and I bird watch together.

       A. It's always a great time at my grandparents' house.
       B. My grandpa is a smart man.
       C. My grandparents know a lot of things.

2.   Think of the benefits of no homework after school. Children could benefit
       from spending longer periods with their families. They could have more
       time for hobbies. They would also be able to see their friends more often.

       A. Kids need a longer recess time.
       B. How could you benefit from no more homework?
       C. More time to do other things is important.

3.   The coolest kid moved into the house down the street. He likes the same
       activities as I do. He is going to go to my homeschool co-op. The best part
       is that he said we can hang out any time he's free.

       A. I can't believe I have an awesome new friend who lives a block away.
       B. We're going to hang out tomorrow.
       C. We have many plans made already.

61

Exercise: Write a Closing Sentence

Read the paragraphs below and add your own closing sentence.

Spaghetti is an excellent dinner to serve when guests come over. It makes a large portion, most people love it, and you can add yummy sides like garlic bread.

Possible answers

There is no going wrong with a dinner like spaghetti.

The Blue Water Bridge is an important piece of architecture. It provides a route of transportation for shipping trucks traveling from the U.S. to Canada. It allows tourists to visit America. It also lets Americans go to Canada and see Niagara Falls.

It may be pretty to look at, but it's actually vital for transportation.

Golden retrievers are a popular family dog. They enjoy being around children. They are generally friendly. They also like to play.

There are many easons why families choose golden retrievers as a pet for their home.

62

Exercise: Write a Closing Sentence

Read the paragraphs below and add your own closing sentence.

Possible answers

Summer camp is a place I look forward to going every year. I see old friends. We go on hikes. There are always crafts, archery, swimming, fishing, and campfires.

Have you considered going to Summer camp this year?

I was worried about starting my first job, but it turned out to be a lot of fun. I learned new skills. I met new people. The job also helped build my confidence, so I won't be as nervous for my next job.

If you feel anxious about starting a new job, just know that the jitters will probably end after the first couple of days.

Everyone is excited about the school dance coming up. There will be a live band. Food and drinks are going to be available. We all have to dress up too.

The whole school will probably be attending the dance.

63

108

Exercise: Write a Closing Sentence

Read the paragraphs below and add your own closing sentence.

Possible answers

The boardwalk is where teenagers like to hang out on summer nights. They park their cars along the river. Some turn the music up loud. Everyone talks and mingles by the parking lot.

Have you ever thought that the boardwalk could be a fun hangout spot?

The Sandusky drive-in is the last standing outdoor theater in Michigan. Every summer, people from all around drive there for the experience. The concession stand has food and drinks. There are two movies that play back to back.

Think about spending an evening at the drive-in before it doesn't exist anymore.

Making candles is a hobby that some crafty people might enjoy. It's a skill that must be learned. You can give them away as gifts. They also make nice decorations for yourself.

Anyone who likes making crafts could find out that they also like candle making as well.

64

Get this workbook next!

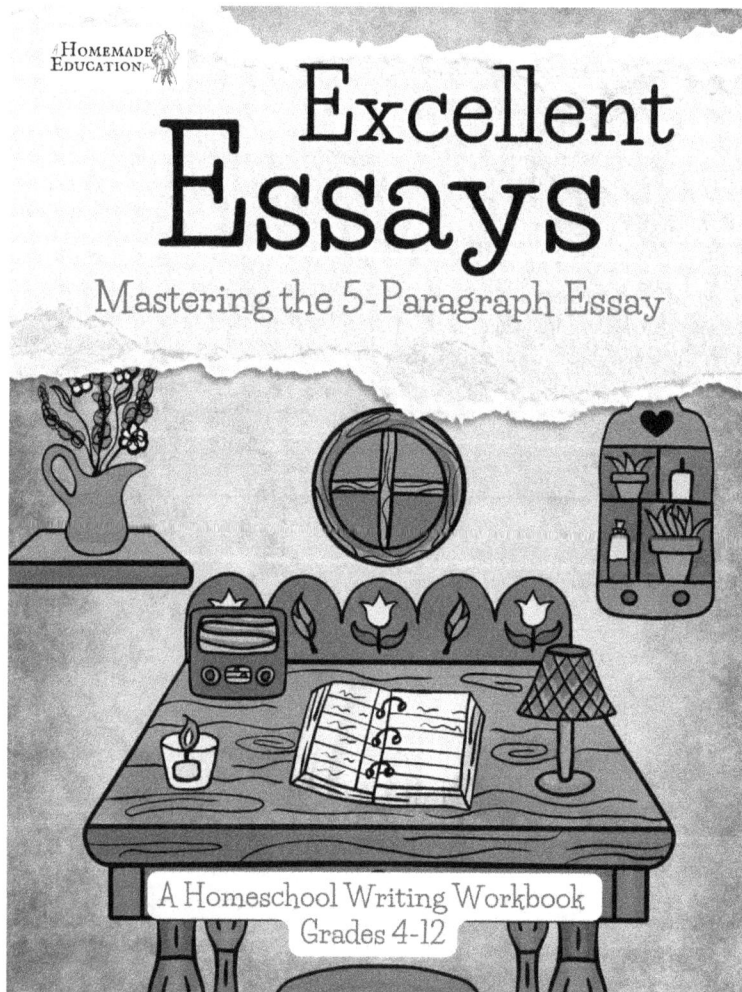

HOMEMADE EDUCATION

Excellent Essays

Mastering the 5-Paragraph Essay

A Homeschool Writing Workbook
Grades 4-12